John Shippen & Oscar Bunn
American Firsts in Golf

Written by
Allison Singh

Illustrated by
Sergio Garzon

It Happened on LI Books
New York
www.ithappenedonli.com
ISBN 978-1-735339535

for Thurman and Ruby Simmons

On July 18, 1896, John Shippen and Oscar Bunn stepped onto the Shinnecock Hills golf course to take on the best golfers in the world.

It was the first U.S. Open tournament held at the Long Island club, and the second in the United States.

Shippen was only sixteen.
Bunn was nineteen.

They were not members of Shinnecock Hills Golf
Club, and never would be. They worked for the club, first
as part of the crew clearing the narrow strip of land
between the Atlantic Ocean and Shinnecock Bay.

Then, when the golf club opened in 1891, Shippen and Bunn stayed on as employees.

The course sat two miles from the Shinnecock Reservation, where both boys lived. As they walked to work, they may have talked about the tasks waiting for them - carrying and cleaning golf clubs, riding wagons to water the grass and chasing raccoons off the greens!

It was the job of caddie that would change their lives and land them in the 1896 U.S. Open. Caddies do not just carry a golfer's clubs. They also offer valuable tips on how to play each hole. To become caddies, the boys had to learn the game of golf and the secrets of the Shinnecock Hills course.

The new club was very popular and needed caddies. Their boss, a golf instructor from Scotland named Willie Dunn, decided to train the boys for the job. Dunn quickly realized they were naturals, with talent far surpassing any club member.

This was particularly true for Shippen, who became Dunn's assistant. He was known for outplaying all of the club members, as well as their guests.

When the newly formed United States Golf Association
(USGA) announced that the 1896 U.S. Open would be held at
Shinnecock Hills Golf Club, the members asked their two best
golfers - Shippen and Bunn - to represent them. This
made teenagers Shippen and Bunn the first American-born
golfers to play in a professional tournament.

Golf was a new sport in America. Professional golfers were
from wealthy families in Scotland and England. They attended
schools like Oxford and trained at the famous St. Andrews
course in Scotland. These golfers dominated the sport and came
to Shinnecock Hills in 1896 expecting to win.

Americans were placing their hopes in Shippen.

One headline described Shippen as "A Golf Caddie Who Is Destined to Become a Champion."

Days before the tournament another newspaper called Shippen "one of the best, if not the best, of all the players."

The New York Herald called him "the boy wonder of golf." Even in England, the press was writing about Shippen's game.

"As a caddie his chance to play is comparatively limited, but John can today beat any amateur in the country, and very probably some of the lesser professionals.
It would not be at all surprising if before long John Shippen...appeared in the open championship as one of the most threatening candidates for honors."

The Windsor Review, June 10, 1896

Shippen and Bunn were ready to show
the world what they could do.

But

they

almost

never

got

the

chance.

On the eve of the tournament, a group of Scottish and
British golfers signed a petition refusing to play
with Shippen and Bunn.

Why?

It wasn't their age,
or lack of money.

It wasn't because they were
employees,
and not club members.

It was their race.

Shippen was Black.

Bunn was Shinnecock.

Suddenly, the 1896 U.S. Open was about more than golf. It was about what golf would look like in America.

The story Americans told about their country was one of liberty and opportunity. This was supposed to set America apart from the kings and queens of Europe.

Yet it was not true for *all* Americans.

Shippen was the grandson of slaves. After the Civil War, his grandparents moved from Virginia to Washington, D.C., where Shippen was born. His father graduated from Howard University and brought the family to Long Island after accepting a position as Presbyterian minister for the Shinnecock Reservation.

Bunn's Shinnecock ancestors had lived on Long Island for centuries. His father was one of ten Shinnecock men who drowned in the rescue mission for the infamous *Circassian* shipwreck off Long Island. The land Bunn was hired to clear for the golf course was a sacred burial ground for Shinnecock people. As Willie Dunn tells it, they "scooped out the burial mounds to make bunkers and sand traps," and sometimes a golf swing would bring up "a bone or two."

The America of 1896 was a segregated society.

Two months before the 1896 U.S. Open, the Supreme Court decided *Plessy v. Ferguson.* This case made "separate but equal" the law of the land.

The law in 1896 did not see Bunn or any other Native American as citizens. This would not change until 1924, years after Bunn's death.

Blacks and Native Americans could not play at white golf clubs, and there were no Black-owned clubs at the time. When local governments started building public golf courses, most were segregated or did not allow non-whites at all.

In this era of segregation, it would not have been surprising for golf to turn its back on Shippen and Bunn, and give in to the demands of the Scottish and British golfers.

But what would the U.S. Open be with no American-born golfers?

There was also the issue of money. The first president of the USGA, Theodore Havemeyer, had invested his own money in the tournament. He and other investors wanted the sport to grow in America, not be disgraced by scandal.

The fate of the tournament was in Havemeyer's hands.

Theodore Havemeyer

That night, he gave the golfers his answer. Shippen and Bunn would play, even if they were the only two golfers in the tournament.

The Scottish and British golfers were shocked and silent. Until the next morning, nobody knew if they would show up.

But they did.

And they were not the only ones. Carriages arrived all day bringing legendary figures from the Gilded Age — Vanderbilts, Mellons, Rothschilds and more. By the afternoon hundreds of men and women were walking the course to follow the action. The scarlet jackets of Shinnecock Hills members dotted the landscape. Shippen's mentor, Willie Dunn, had moved away, but returned to play in the U.S. Open.

Shippen's partner was more than double his age. His name was Charles Blair MacDonald, winner of the U.S. Amateur tournament the year before. MacDonald was born in Canada and raised in Chicago, but learned golf in Scotland at the famous University of St. Andrews. Unlike Shippen, he was a member of Shinnecock Hills Golf Club.

The tournament consisted of thirty six holes - eighteen in the morning and another eighteen in the afternoon. During the lunch break players compared scores. Guess who was tied for the lead?

John Shippen!

Shippen scored 78 and was tied with his old mentor, Willie Dunn. Oscar Bunn scored 89. Charles MacDonald finished the morning round twelve strokes behind Shippen and withdrew from the tournament. He spent the afternoon following Shippen, keeping his score.

After lunch, excitement was in the air. Shippen left
no doubt he could play with the best in the world, but
could he win?

He remained tied for first place until the thirteenth
hole, where he hit the ball too far right onto a sandy path.

The ball was stuck. Shippen swung, then again, but the ball just rolled along the path. He could not lift it into the air with his club.

Today's golfers use the sand wedge for these tricky shots, but it had not yet been invented in 1896!

It took eleven strokes for Shippen's ball to finally drop in the hole. It was too many strokes to win the tournament. Many people agree that if not for that one hole, John Shippen would have won the 1896 U.S. Open.

With an overall score of 159, Shippen tied for fifth place with H.J. Whigham, the current U.S. Amateur champion. Willie Dunn finished behind Shippen with a score of 165, and Oscar Bunn finished with a 174.

OPEN CHAMPIONSHIP—1896

HELD AT SHINNECOCK HILLS, JULY 18

Thirty-six holes, medal play.

James Foulis, Chicago	78,	74—152
H. Rawlins, Sadaquada	79,	76—155
G. Douglas, Brookline	79,	79—158
John Shippen, Shinnecock Hills	78,	81—159
Mr. A. W. Smith, Toronto	78,	80—158
Mr. H. J. Whigham, Onwentsia	82,	77—159
Joe Lloyd, Essex	78,	82—160
W. Tucker, St. Andrews	78,	82—160
R. B. Wilson, Shinnecock Hills	82,	80—162
A. Ricketts, Albany	80,	83—163
W. H. Way, Meadowbrook	83,	81—164
W. Dunn, Ardsley	78,	87—165
W. F. Davis, Newport	83,	84—167
John Harrison, Ridgefield	92,	91—183
J. Patrick, Tuxedo	86,	86—172
W. Campbell, Myopia	85,	85—170
A. Patrick, Tuxedo	88,	85—173
W. Norton, Lakewood	87,	98—185
T. Warrender, Knollwood	97,	93—190
R. Anderson, Westbrook	92,	95—187
John Reid, Philadelphia C. C.	88,	84—172
W. T. Hoare, Philadelphia Cricket	90,	81—171
J. I. Anson, Westbrook	88,	92—180
Tom Gourley, Baltusrol	82,	91—173
W. W. Campbell, Philadelphia	91,	93—184
G. Strath, Dyker Meadow	91,	89—180
J. N. Mackrell, Essex	89,	83—172
Oscar Bunn, Shinnecock Hills	89,	85—174

Did not finish: Mr. C. B. Macdonald, Chicago; E. A. Wilkie, Newton Centre; Daniel Leitch, Denver; James Dagleish, Shinnecock Hills; Samuel Tucker, St. Andrews.

The Official Golf Guide for 1900, Josiah Newman

Even though he did not win, Shippen's play left the crowd astonished. He finished to applause and hugs from his Shinnecock friends.

Newspaper reports placed him "among the very best players of the game on either continent." *The Chicago Tribune* described Shippen as "the most remarkable player in the United States."

After the tournament, Shippen faced a major life decision. Would he pursue a college degree like his father and siblings? They had graduated from Howard, Yale and Oberlin, and wanted Shippen to follow this path.

Golf was a sport for the wealthy and white. Shippen was neither, but had talent and loved the game.

Could that be enough?

Shippen followed his heart.

He accepted a position as golf professional at the Maidstone Club in Easthampton, NY. He gave lessons, competed in tournaments and sold golf clubs he made himself. Shippen played in four more U.S. Open tournaments - 1899, 1900, 1902 and 1913. His best finish was fifth place in the 1902 U.S. Open at Long Island's Garden City Golf Club.

Shippen and the Maidstone manager Kenneth Davis, who was white, turned segregated society upside down when Davis caddied for Shippen in local tournaments.

Bunn did not enter another U.S. Open, but continued to teach golf and work at golf clubs.

In 1901, the *Brooklyn Daily Eagle* featured Bunn and his advice on the perfect swing.

Bunn's career was cut short in 1918 when he died from pneumonia at the age of 41.

Shippen and Bunn proved that talent is color blind. Unfortunately, the world of golf was not.

In 1916, the Professional Golfers' Association of America (PGA) was formed. This organization only invited white players to tournaments, even if non-whites qualified to play.

Then, in 1934, the PGA officially segregated the sport by amending its bylaws to include the "Caucasians only" clause. Non-Whites were barred from PGA events, as well as the cash prizes, sponsorships and recognition that came with them.

After Shippen's last U.S. Open in 1913, no Black golfer competed in the U.S. Open for another thirty-five years.

USGA Caucasian Clause

"Male professional golfers of the Caucasian race, over the age of eighteen years (18), residing in North or South America, who can qualify under the terms and conditions hereinafter specified, shall be eligible for membership or 'H' Apprentice status."

Around this time, Black golfers formed the United Golfers Association (UGA) and held tournaments of their own. Unlike the PGA, the UGA was open to all races.

The best golfers in the world still wanted to test their skills against Shippen, but how could they when tournaments and golf courses were closed to Blacks?

The only way possible.

They snuck him in.

In 1931 John Shippen found his home at the first Black-owned golf club in the U.S., Shady Rest Golf and Country Club.

At this club in Scotch Plains, New Jersey, Blacks could freely play golf, tennis and other sports. They also dined, socialized and enjoyed life with legends like Duke Ellington, W.E.B. DuBois, Ella Fitzgerald and Billie Holiday. Althea Gibson, the first female Black tennis player to win Wimbledon and the U.S. Open, was also a regular at Shady Rest.

Shippen was beloved by the Shady Rest members and their children. He taught many youngsters to love the game of golf, despite its flaws. Shippen worked at Shady Rest for over thirty years and retired in 1960.

One year later, the PGA finally lifted its ban on non-white members.

At the age of ninety, John Shippen died in a nursing home in Newark, New Jersey. He was buried in an unmarked grave.

Many years later, a man named Thurman Simmons heard Shippen's story and went searching for his burial spot. It wasn't easy. He walked for hours until he found it - a small plate in the ground marked with the number 71.

Simmons replaced the plate with a proper headstone, and has worked tirelessly with his wife Ruby to give John Shippen his rightful place in history as America's first professional golfer.

Near the end of his life, Shippen wondered if choosing golf over college was the right decision.

"I wonder until I look out the window and see that golf course," he said. "Then I realize how much enjoyment I've gotten out of the game, and I don't wonder anymore."

Shippen was admitted into the PGA in 2009, four decades after his death.

<u>**Afterword**</u>

Oscar Bunn was inducted into the Caddie Hall of Fame in 2009. After protests by the Shinnecock Nation at the 2018 U.S. Open at Shinnecock Hills, the USGA announced plans for the Oscar Bunn Tribal Golf Facility on the grounds of the Shinnecock Reservation. The 6,500 square foot facility was opened in 2019.

Many accounts of Shippen's life incorrectly state that he was of Shinnecock heritage. Both of Shippen's wives were Shinnecock, which could be one explanation for the error. It has also been suggested that Havemeyer falsely told the Scottish and British golfers that Shippen was half Shinnecock to ease their racial concerns.

Theodore Havemeyer died of typhoid fever one year after the 1896 U.S. Open. His name is still on the U.S. Open championship trophy. Charles MacDonald went on to design numerous golf courses, including a hole at Shinnecock Hills. He joined with H.J. Whigham to design the National Golf Links of America in Southampton, NY. H.J. Whigham served as the editor of *Town & Country* magazine for twenty-five years, and died in Southampton.

Thurman and Ruby Simmons created and run the John Shippen Memorial Golf Foundation, Inc. Over the years, this non-profit organization has given scholarships and held golf tournaments and clinics for young people. You can learn more about the foundation's work at <u>https:// www.johnshippenmemorialgolffoundation.com</u>. The Shady Rest Golf & Country Club clubhouse was preserved through the hard work of the Simmons, Sylvia Hicks and Scotch Plains community leaders. A small museum in the clubhouse is dedicated to sharing John Shippen's story with the public.

John Shippen (second from left) finishing in second place at the African American
United Golfers Association tournament at Shady Rest Golf Club in 1925

Headstone for John Shippen

Oscar Bunn

John Shippen

Sources

Articles

"A Golf Caddie Who is Destined to Become a Champion." *Windsor Review*, June 10, 1896.

Alvarez, Anya. "At the Height of her Tennis Career, Althea Gibson Turned to Golf." Boston: WBUR, December 22, 2017. https://www.wbur.org/onlyagame/2017/12/22/althea-gibson-golf.

Carrico, Nicole. "Open History: University of South Carolina holds only known film footage of first American pro golfer John Shippen." SC.edu, June 14, 2018. https://www.sc.edu/uofsc/posts/2018/06/shippen_movietone_footage.php#0.

Brown, Leonard. "'The Mecca' Shady Rest Golf & Country Club." *African American Golfer's Digest*, February 2, 2021.

Dear, Tony. "The Story Behind Shinnecock Hills." *Golf World*, June 10, 2018.

Denney, Bob. "From Caddie to Pro: America's First Home-Grown Golf Pro, John M. Shippen." *PGA.com*, February 5, 2018. https://www.pga.com/archive/pga-of-america/pga-feature/black-history-month-americas-first-home-grown-golf-pro-john-shippen-jr.

Dunn, Willie. "Early Courses of the United States." *Golf Illustrated*, September 1934.

"Fowlis was Best Golfer." *The New York Times*, July 19, 1896.

Greene, Baylis, "The Brief Golfing Life of Oscar Bunn." *The Southampton Review*, Summer 2015.

"John Shippen - A Golfing Pioneer." *USGA.org*, February 10, 2016. https://www.usga.org/articles/2016/02/john-shippen--a-golfing-pioneer.html.

Kirsch, George B. "Municipal Golf and Civil Rights in the United States, 1910-1965." *The Journal of African American History*, vol. 92, no. 3, 2007.

"Oscar Bunn Obituary." *Southampton Press*, January 1918.

"Shinnecock Indian Expert Tells How Golf Should be Played." *The Brooklyn Daily Eagle*, October 20, 1901.

"Shippen Beats Wilson." *The Brooklyn Daily Eagle*, August 28, 1896.

St. Laurent, Philip. "The Negro in World History - John Shippen." *Tuesday Magazine - The Oakland Tribune*, April 5, 1969.

Steves, Peter F. "Shippen Broke Down a Barrier." *Golf Journal*, Feb 13, 1997.

"The Great American Golfer." *Kokomo Daily Tribune*, May 20, 1896.

VanHouten, Matt. "John Matthew Shippen, Jr." *Black Past*, February 21, 2011. https://www.blackpast.org/african-american-history/shippen-john-matthew-jr-1879-1968/.

Vohden, Danny. "Oscar Bunn Facility Brings Pride to Shinnecock Nation." *USGA.org*, September 16, 2020. https://www.usga.org/content/usga/home-page/articles/2020/09/oscar-bunn-facility-brings-pride-to-shinnecock-nation.html.

Books

Demas, Lane. *Game of Privilege - An African American History of Golf.* Chapel Hill: University of North Carolina Press, 2017.

Eikleberry, Sara Jane. "Chapter One: John M. Shippen, Jr. - Testing the Front Nine of American Golf," *Before Jackie Robinson - The Transcendent Role of Black Sporting Pioneers*. Lincoln: University of Nebraska Press, 2017.

McDaniel, Pete. *Uneven Lies - The Heroic Stories of African Americans in Golf.* United States: The American Golfer, Inc., 2000.

Newman, Josiah. *The Official Golf Guide for 1900.* Garden City: Harper's, 1900.

Sinnette, Calvin, H. *Forbidden Fairways - African Americans and the Game of Golf.* Baltimore: Black Classic Press, 2015.

Slovic, Lyle. "Chapter Five - John R. Shippen, Jr. 'The Father of African-American Golf,'" *Shadows on the Green: Golf's Scandals, Tragedies, Triumphs and Offbeat Tales.* United States: Lulu.com Publishing, 2020.

<u>Documentaries</u>

Uneven Fairways - The Story of the Negro Leagues of Golf. Moxie Pictures, 2009.

John Shippen at African American United Golfers Association Tournament. Fox Movietone News Collection at the University of South Carolina, 1925.

About the Author

Allison Singh first learned about John Shippen by accident while researching another topic on the website Blackpast.org. She was immediately drawn to the Long Island story of John Shippen and Oscar Bunn set against the backdrop of segregated society at the turn of the century. Allison is also the author of *MLK & LI: Martin Luther King, Jr., and Long Island*.

About the Illustrator

Artist Sergio Garzon was born in Bogota, Colombia and lives and works in Honolulu, Hawaii. As a professional illustrator, Garzon has been featured on NPR's "All Things Considered," *The Honolulu Star Advertiser* and television networks covering his street art. He has fifteen years of experience in hand-drawn design and illustration.

Ways to Support

John Shippen Memorial Golf Foundation, Inc.
https://www.johnshippenmemorialgolffoundation.com
On Facebook: @JohnShippenMemorialGolfFoundation

Shinnecock Golfers Association Scholarship Fund
PO Box 2028
Southampton, NY 11969-2028

www.ingramcontent.com/pod-product-compliance
Lightning Source LLC
Chambersburg PA
CBHW082246060726
47598CB00017B/2858